W9-AHY-750

ASPCA

PET CARE GUIDES FOR KIDS

GUINEA PIGS

Mark Evans

DORLING KINDERSLEY, INC.

NEW YORK

6181671

A DORLING KINDERSLEY BOOK

For my brother, Andrew

Project Editor Liza Bruml
Art Editor Jane Coney
Editor Miriam Farbey
Designer Rebecca Johns
U.S. Editor B. Alison Weir
Photographer Paul Bricknell
Illustrator Malcolm McGregor
ASPCA Consultant Stephen Zawistowski, Ph.D.

First American Edition, 1992
10 9 8 7 6 5 4 3 2 1

Published in the United States by
Dorling Kindersley, Inc., 232 Madison Avenue
New York, New York 10016

Copyright © 1992 Dorling Kindersley Limited, London
Text copyright © 1992 Mark Evans
Foreword © 1992 Roger Caras

All rights reserved under International and Pan-American Copyright
Conventions. No part of this publication may be reproduced, stored
in a retrieval system, or transmitted in any form or by any means,
electronic, mechanical, photocopying, recording, or otherwise,
without the prior written permission of the copyright owner.
Published in Great Britain by Dorling Kindersley Limited.
Distributed by Houghton Mifflin Company, Boston.

Library of Congress Cataloging-in-Publication Data
Evans, Mark, 1962-
    Guinea pigs / Mark Evans. — 1st American ed.
    p. cm. — (ASPCA pet care guides for kids)
    Includes index.
    Summary: Offers information for the first-time pet owner on
the physical characteristics, selection, care, and feeding of guinea
pigs.
    ISBN 1-56458-125-X
    1. Guinea pigs as pets—Juvenile literature. [1. Guinea pigs.
2. Pets.] I. Title. II. Series.
SF459.G9E82 1992
636' .93234—dc20   92-52826
                                                CIP
                                                AC

Color reproduction by Colourscan, Singapore
Printed and bound by Arnoldo Mondadori, Verona, Italy

Models: Narada Bernard, Jacob Brubert, Jade Carrington, Martin Cooles,
Laura Douglas, Angelina Halkou, Louisa Hall, Thanh Huynh,
Gupreet Janday, Rachel Mamauag, Paul Mitchell, Serena Palmer,
Florence Prowen, Isabel Prowen, Jamie Sallon, Lisa Wardropper

Dorling Kindersley would like to thank Peter Gurney for supplying guinea
pigs, Wood Green Animal Shelters, The Cambridge Cavy Trust,
Bridget Hopkinson for editorial help, Christopher Howson for design help,
Salvo Tomasselli for the world map, and Lynn Bresler for the index.

Picture credits: Walter Büchi p12 tl, tr; Steve Shott p25 c

Foreword

There is a wonderful collection of animals
called "shelf pets." These are animals that
can't really have the free run of our homes,
but can still be good companions. You
shouldn't have a shelf pet, or any other
pet, unless you are going to learn about
them and care about them. In a very real
way, your pets are your infant children.
They will return affection for affection,
and all kinds of nice feelings for good and
gentle care. Just as you and I want to be
protected and
loved, so do
they, and
that's your job.

Roger Caras *ASPCA President*

Note to parents

This book teaches your child how to be
a caring and responsible pet owner. But
remember, your child must have your
help and guidance in every aspect of
day-to-day pet care. Don't let your child
keep guinea pigs unless you are sure that
your family has the time and resources
to care for them properly—for the whole
of their lives.

Contents

Introduction

The first step to becoming a good guinea pig owner is to choose the right kind and number of pets. Guinea pigs with short hair are the easiest to care for. A guinea pig likes to have company, so you should get at least two. But remember, whatever kinds and however many pets you choose, you'll need to care for them every day. Not just to start with, but for the whole of their lives.

Shopping basket full of supplies you will need

Understanding your pets

You have to get to know your guinea pigs. If you handle them gently and talk to them as much as you can, they will quickly learn to trust you. Watch them very carefully, and you will soon begin to understand the many fascinating ways that they talk to each other.

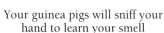

Your guinea pigs will sniff your hand to learn your smell

Caring for your pets

You will be your pets' best friend only if you care for them properly. You will need to make sure that they eat the right foods, always have water, and get plenty of exercise every day. You will also have to groom them regularly, and keep their hutch clean.

You will have to groom your guinea pigs every day

Things to do with your pets

Your guinea pigs are very active. You should play with them in their fun box and enclosure every day. If you keep them busy, you will show everyone that you are a good pet owner.

Hiding food is a favorite game

People to help

The best guinea pig owner always tries to find out more about her pets. You can ask your veterinarian how to keep your guinea pigs healthy and happy.

You will need to visit your veterinarian regularly

New family members

Your guinea pigs will be a very special part of your whole family. Everyone will want to pet them, and be interested in what they do. They can even become good friends with some of your other pets.

Ask a grown-up
⚥ When you see this sign, you should ask an adult to help you.

Your pets will become part of your family

Things to remember

When you keep guinea pigs, there are some important rules you must always follow:

❖ Wash your hands after petting or playing with your pets, and after cleaning their hutch.

❖ Don't kiss your guinea pigs.

❖ Never give your guinea pigs food from your plate.

❖ If your guinea pigs are hiding or in their beds, don't annoy them.

❖ Never tease your guinea pigs.

❖ Always watch your guinea pigs when they are with other pets.

❖ Never, ever hit your guinea pigs.

What is a guinea pig?

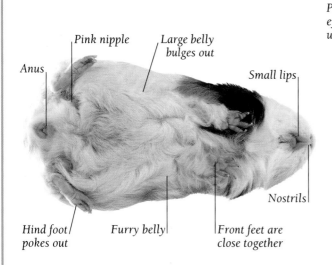 A guinea pig is not really a pig at all. It is a rodent, and its correct name is a cavy. Rodents have very sharp front teeth that never stop growing. They are used for gnawing. All rodents belong to a group of animals called mammals. Mammals have warm blood and a hairy body. When young, they drink milk from their mothers.

Small and tubby
A guinea pig has a plump body. It has short legs, so it is not good at running a long way or climbing. A guinea pig's neck is very short and its mouth is very near the ground, so it doesn't have to bend down to graze on grass.

Anus

Pink nipple

Large belly bulges out

Small lips

Nostrils

Hind foot pokes out

Furry belly

Front feet are close together

Protruding eyebrows are used to feel

Long whiskers bristle out to feel

Sharp claws grip securely on rough ground

Underneath your guinea pig
A guinea pig has a great big stomach where tough plant food is digested. It is so large that the back legs have to point sideways to fit around it. The front feet are close together and lift the head off the ground. Look closely at the belly and you will see two nipples. In a mother guinea pig, they are sucked for milk by her babies.

Ear hears the
faintest sounds

Eye keeps
watch for
enemies

Nose detects
the weakest
of smells

Whiskers sense
danger around face

Large mouth
has room for
20 teeth

Always alert
A guinea pig can detect
danger, even when eating
with its head down. It
has good hearing and a
very keen sense of smell.
Its eyes are on the sides
of its head, so it can tell
if something creeps up
from behind.

**Look closer
at your
guinea pig**

Eyelids clean
dust from the eye
when the guinea
pig blinks.

The front teeth
keep growing.
Gnawing grinds
them down.

The big back foot
has three toes and
a leathery sole.

The front foot
has four toes.
Leathery pads
protect the fine
toe bones.

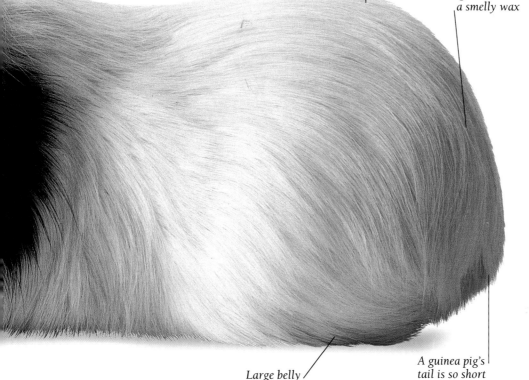

Thick, furry coat helps keep
the guinea pig warm

Grease gland makes
a smelly wax

Large belly
hides back legs

A guinea pig's
tail is so short
you can't see it

When a guinea
pig stands up,
you can see its
long back legs.

Life in the wild

Wild guinea pigs live in family groups in the high mountains and the flat grasslands of South America. A long time ago, they were bred for food by the local people. Traders took wild guinea pigs from South America all over the world. The guinea pigs that we keep today as pets are descended from these wild guinea pigs.

Natural home
Wild guinea pigs trample down the grass around their homes to make paths, called runways. They live in the tall grass, or in the old burrows of other animals.

Wild ancestor
The wild guinea pig is smaller and has a more pointed snout than the domestic guinea pig. Its coarse fur may be brown, black, or gray. Each hair has a light tip that makes the coat look speckled.

Tall, dry grass is easy to flatten

Guinea pig looks out curiously

Guinea pig sits in hollowed-out grass runway

Guinea pig likes to hide away

Hiding away

Guinea pigs are very timid. They spend a lot of time hiding in grass. They sleep for about five hours a day, but they never close their eyes for more than ten minutes!

Guinea pig's favorite pastime is nibbling

Nibbling morning and evening

Guinea pigs eat for about six hours every day. They feed in dim light, mainly at dawn and dusk, when their enemies find it difficult to see them.

Friendly group

When they are not eating or sleeping, guinea pigs like to be with their families and friends. They huddle together, play, and go exploring.

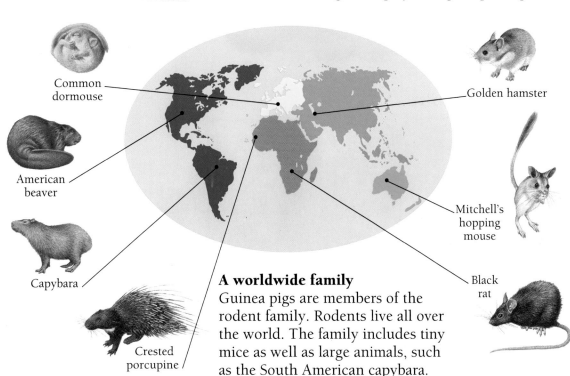

Common dormouse

Golden hamster

American beaver

Capybara

Mitchell's hopping mouse

Black rat

Crested porcupine

A worldwide family

Guinea pigs are members of the rodent family. Rodents live all over the world. The family includes tiny mice as well as large animals, such as the South American capybara.

All colors and patterns

There are many kinds, or breeds, of guinea pigs. Some have a single-colored coat. These are called "self" types. "Non-self" types have up to three colors in their coats. Guinea pigs also have different hair styles— short, long, tufty, and wiry. Think carefully before choosing guinea pigs with long hair. Their shaggy coats need a lot of extra care.

Hairs have light tips

Non-self agouti and orange

Agouti guinea pigs
The hair on agoutis changes in color from the root to the tip. This makes them look speckled. All wild guinea pigs are agoutis.

Shiny coat is orange

Black bottom

White band around middle

Black patch

Brown patch

Short-haired guinea pigs
Short-haired guinea pigs have a smooth, glossy coat. The coat patterns have names, such as Dutch and tortoiseshell.

White patch

Non-self Dutch

Self golden

White stripe

Non-self tortoiseshell and white

Ridge along spine

Fur stands on end

Brown tuft on head

Self white Abyssinian

Non-self tortoiseshell and white Abyssinian

Abyssinian guinea pigs
All the hair on your head grows from one center that is called a hair crown. Abyssinian, or rough-coated guinea pigs, have many hair crowns all over their bodies. This makes their coats look very tufty.

Non-self tortoiseshell Abyssinian

Coat is made up of swirls of black and orange hair

Crowning crests

Some guinea pigs have a special hair crown on the top of their heads. This is called a crest.

Golden crest

Non-self crested Dalmatian

Self crested ruby

How a guinea pig gets its looks

Two guinea pigs of the same breed produce an identical pig.

The pup looks the same as its parents.

Two different breeds of guinea pigs produce a mix, or crossbred.

The pup looks a little like both of its parents.

Two crossbred pigs can have pups with a variety of colorings.

A real mixture!

Long, soft hair

Non-self Peruvians

Peruvians

Peruvian guinea pigs have silky hair that grows down to the ground. The fringe must be brushed back to keep it from covering their eyes.

Gray and white hair is short on face

Non-self Sheltie

Shaggy Shelties

Shelties have very long coats, but their hair does not grow over their faces. They can see where they are going more easily than Peruvians.

White coat with brown spots

Silky fur feels smooth

Silky satins

Some guinea pigs have very soft and shiny fur. These are called satins.

Non-self Dalmatian satin

Self ruby satin

Non-self agouti rex

Wavy rexes

Rex guinea pigs have short, thick hair. Their wavy coats feel coarse when you pet them.

Self ruby rex

Non-self Dutch rex

Your guinea pigs' home

Before you bring your guinea pigs home, you must get a hutch for them. They are very active, so the hutch must have plenty of space. Put the hutch in a sheltered place, where it is safe from other animals. Remember to stock up with guinea pig food (see p. 26). You will also need bedding and feeding equipment.

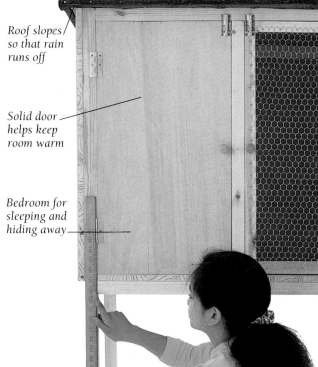

Roof slopes so that rain runs off

Solid door helps keep room warm

Bedroom for sleeping and hiding away

Check the size of the hutch before you buy

A branch from a fruit tree, such as apple

Sheets of paper
You need some large pieces of paper to line the floor of the hutch. Old drawing paper or newspaper is ideal.

Shredded paper
Buy shredded paper bedding. Your guinea pigs will make their beds in the soft paper.

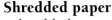

Hay
Get some dry, fresh hay. Guinea pigs love to eat hay and will also use it to make their beds.

Gnawing log
Find a small, untreated fruit tree branch for your guinea pigs to gnaw on. Gnawing helps keep their teeth healthy.

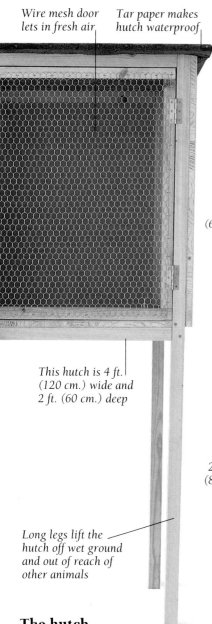

Wire mesh door lets in fresh air

Tar paper makes hutch waterproof

Food container
You need a container to store your guinea pigs' food.

Airtight box keeps food fresh

Heavy bowl is hard to tip over

Make sure cats and wild animals can't get into the hutch.

2 ft. (60 cm.)

Food bowls
You will need two small bowls. But don't get plastic because your guinea pigs may gnaw them.

Your guinea pigs will get too hot in bright sunshine.

This hutch is 4 ft. (120 cm.) wide and 2 ft. (60 cm.) deep

Water bottle
Buy a water bottle with a dropper. The dropper lets out water when a guinea pig sucks the end of the metal tube.

Shelter the hutch from wind and rain.

2 ½ ft. (80 cm.)

Long legs lift the hutch off wet ground and out of reach of other animals

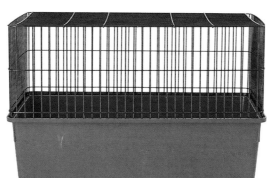

Your guinea pigs will freeze if left out in the bitter cold.

The hutch
❖ Look at the measurements in the picture. Your pets' hutch should be at least this big. The hutch should have two rooms. The large room is used for eating. The smaller room is used as a bedroom. Your guinea pigs will make their beds and hide in it.

A home for indoor guinea pigs
You can keep your pigs indoors. They need a small cage to sleep in. Make them a fun box to play and eat in when they are awake.

Put the hutch in a place where you can look at it often.

Things you will need

You will need to get some special items to help you care for your new pets. Do not put anything made of plastic in their hutch or fun box, because your guinea pigs will chew everything. Make sure you have gotten all your supplies ready before you pick up your guinea pigs.

Air hole

Carrying box
Ask your veterinarian for a pet carrying box in which to carry your guinea pigs. It should have holes to let in air so your guinea pigs can breathe.

Towel   Water jug   Shampoo

Hot water bottle   Dishpan

Squeaky clean
Sometimes you will need to wash your guinea pigs. Buy special shampoo. Find an old dishpan to use as a bathtub and a jug to pour water. You will need a towel to dry your pets, and a hot water bottle to keep them warm as they dry.

Brush has soft bristles

Comb with rounded prongs

Brush and comb
Your guinea pigs' hair may become tangled. Buy a small, soft brush and fine comb to help you untangle it.

Brush   Comb

Weighing tray

Kitchen scale
You will need to weigh your guinea pigs on a kitchen scale to check that they are healthy. Line the tray with paper.

Cleaning equipment

To clean your guinea pigs' hutch, you will need special items. Never take items that are used to clean your house. Ask your veterinarian which type of disinfectant spray to buy. Keep the cleaning equipment together, so it is not used to clean anything else.

The fun box

You can make an indoor fun box for your guinea pigs and fill it with things for them to play with. Playing in the fun box will keep your pets fit and happy if you can't let them outdoors.

Dish washing liquid   Disinfectant spray   Bucket

Rubber gloves   Brush   Dustpan

Scrubbing brush   Scraper   Bottle brush   Spout brush   Cleaning cloth

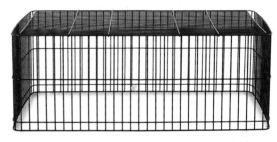

Indoor cage lid

If you keep your guinea pigs indoors, you should occasionally let them outdoors so they can eat grass. Put the top of their cage over them so they can't run away.

Grazing ark

Make or buy a grazing ark so that your guinea pigs can run around and graze outdoors. The ark must have a shaded area so they can shelter from the sun or hide if they are scared.

Choosing your guinea pigs

You should get at least two guinea pigs, because they get lonely if they live alone. The guinea pigs must be the same sex. Get adults that live together already, or choose babies from a litter when they are at least six weeks old. If you want to keep lots of pigs, choose females. More than two boys together will fight.

Five-week-old pup

Well-groomed adult

Babies or adults?
It is easy to fall in love with tiny baby guinea pigs. These are called puppies. But remember, they will soon grow up. Adult guinea pigs can be just as adorable.

Where to find your new guinea pigs
❀ A friend's guinea pig may have babies.
❀ A breeder will sell you a breed of pig.
❀ An animal shelter may have guinea pigs of all kinds that need new homes.

Short hair is easy to care for

Long hair must be brushed regularly

Long hair or short hair?
Long-haired guinea pigs look fancy but their coats need lots of special care. The coats of short-haired guinea pigs don't get so tangled.

Look for lively guinea pigs that like to play

Owner points at the babies

Mother nibbles on cucumber

Shy pup hides

Bold pup explores the coconut shell

1 **When you go to choose** a baby guinea pig, don't touch any of the puppies at first. Watch with the owner from a place where you won't disturb the puppies.

2 Ask the owner to pick up the baby that seems liveliest. Ask whether it is a boy or a girl. Also check that the guinea pig hasn't been chosen by someone else.

Watch to see if the pup is friendly

Pet the pup gently

This curious young guinea pig looks out

Timid pup snuggles up to its mother

Shoe box makes a good hiding place

3 The owner will let you hold the puppy. Make sure you are sitting down. Hold the baby close to your chest so it feels safe. Now decide if you really like it.

Put one hand over the back

Put your other hand underneath the pup's bottom

Look to see if the guinea pig has clear eyes

Feel the fur—it should be soft

4 Check that the guinea pig is healthy. It should have a plump, well-fed body. It should have bright eyes and a clean nose and ears. Its fur should be shiny and silky all over, including under its bottom.

Welcome home

Your guinea pig may be frightened when it first leaves its mother. If you get two babies, they will keep each other company. If you already have a guinea pig and are introducing a new friend, watch carefully when they first meet. Have the hutch ready to help all your pets settle down together.

Veterinarian listens to guinea pig's heartbeat through his stethoscope

Visiting your veterinarian

You should arrange to visit your veterinarian on the way home from picking up your new guinea pig. The veterinarian will examine it to make sure it is healthy. Your veterinarian will be able to answer any questions that you have about your new pet.

Veterinarian looks to find out the sex

Male guinea pig

Female guinea pig

Checking the sex

When a guinea pig is very young, it can be hard to tell whether it is a male or a female. Ask your veterinarian to check the sex, so you are sure it is the sex you wanted.

Male and female

These pictures will help you find out the sex of your guinea pig. Look underneath, between its back legs.

Handling your pet

This chart tells you when to handle your new pets during the first two weeks.

Day 1: Watch your pets, but don't disturb them.

Day 2: Your guinea pigs may hide in their beds. Talk to them, so they get used to your voice.

Day 3: Offer your pets food from your hand. Try to pick them up. Hold on firmly if they wriggle.

Days 4 – 7: Stroke and brush your pets. Show them to your family, and to other pets.

Days 8 – 11: Let your guinea pigs explore their outdoor enclosure, grazing ark, and fun box.

After 2 weeks: Play with your pets every day.

Your guinea pig's home

Everything your pet needs should be in the hutch: bedding, food, water, and a gnawing log. Put your new guinea pig into the hutch and leave it to explore its new home.

Fill the bedroom with shredded paper and hay

Bolt the door after you put the pig in the hutch

Spread hay for food and to make into bed

Attach the bottle, filled with fresh water, to the door

Line the floor with a layer of paper

Bowl should be filled with fresh food

Open the door wide, so you can reach every area

23

Friends for your guinea pigs

Just like you, your guinea pigs like to have a lot of friends. Don't worry if they scuttle off to hide when you try to pick them up. Your guinea pigs are not being unfriendly—just shy. Another guinea pig makes the best friend for your guinea pig. But you, your family, and some other pets all make good guinea pig friends.

Guinea pig feels safe close to its friends

In good company
You can keep lots of female guinea pigs together. Guinea pigs hate to be on their own. They never stray far from each other when they are eating. When they sleep, they huddle together. This keeps them warm.

Introducing a newcomer
When you choose a new friend for your guinea pigs, be careful. Remember that females in a group, or a male on its own, will fight a new adult. It is always best to introduce a new guinea pig that is about six weeks old.

Adult pig sniffs new baby

Baby pig looks timid

Keeping male guinea pigs
You must not keep more than two male guinea pigs together in a hutch. A group of males will fight. Choose two baby males from the same litter. If you already have a male, get it a male friend that is about six weeks old.

This male guinea pig gets along with its brother

Watch the animals all the time

Meeting the family dog

👫 Always ask an adult if you can let your guinea pig meet a dog. A quiet dog will not usually harm your guinea pig, but keep a firm grip on the dog's collar. Never leave them alone together.

Be ready to pick your guinea pig up

Make sure the dog lies down

Friend or foe?

A rabbit can sometimes be friends with a guinea pig. But they may also fight. When a rabbit is annoyed with a guinea pig, it may kick it. A rabbit's back legs are very strong and the kick will hurt badly. Never, ever, keep a rabbit and a guinea pig in the same hutch.

Powerful back legs can kick out

Sharp claws

Part of the family

Show your family and friends how to hold your guinea pigs properly (see p. 21). They love being petted on a lap. Don't leave your pets alone with a younger brother or sister.

Guinea pig feels safe cradled on a lap

Let your baby brother stroke your pet while you hold it

Always sit down to hold a guinea pig

Feeding your guinea pigs

Guinea pigs are herbivores, which means that they only eat grass and plants. In the wild, they eat seeds and wild grasses. To keep your pets fit, you must feed them the same kinds of things. You should give them specially prepared guinea pig food and fresh food (see p. 28). Feed only small amounts of any new type of food.

Razor-sharp front teeth bite off portions of food

Side teeth grind food

Mouth made for chewing
The food your guinea pigs eat needs to be very well chewed. A guinea pig's teeth and mouth are specially made for biting and grinding. The food is mixed with spit in the mouth while it is ground by the teeth.

Dry mix

Dry fiber food

Grazing all day
Grass and some wild plants are favorite foods for guinea pigs. They have to eat a lot of greens to get enough nutrients. Given the chance, your guinea pig will spend most of the day nibbling.

Special foods
Even if your guinea pigs graze on grass, you need to give them other food. They love hay, which is dried grass. You must also buy them special foods made from mixtures of dried plants, seeds, and vegetables.

Hay

A guinea pig spends a lot of time eating

When to feed your guinea pigs
Feed your pets every morning and evening. Guinea pigs must always have dry food to eat. They don't make a store of food, like squirrels or hamsters.

☺ Eating droppings

Don't worry if you see your guinea pigs eating their own droppings—all guinea pigs do this. Their stomachs can't take out all the nutrients from the food the first time they eat it. So they make soft droppings, which they eat again.

Fresh water

Wild guinea pigs get water from the fresh food they eat. Your guinea pigs eat a lot of dry food, so you must make sure their water bottle is always full.

Fasten the bottle where the guinea pigs can easily reach it

Tip of tube has a little ball to stop water from dripping when not in use

Tongue licks the tube tip to make the water flow

Screw lid on tightly

Pour new food into bowl morning and evening

Cheeks suck in when gnawing

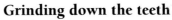

Apple tree log is best

Grinding down the teeth

Wild guinea pigs gnaw trees in order to wear down their ever-growing teeth. This helps to keep their teeth short. Give your pets a log to gnaw. This will stop their teeth from growing too long.

How much do guinea pigs eat?

Each time you feed your guinea pigs, fill the bowls to the brim. Your pets will only eat as much food as they need. If they have plenty of exercise, they won't get fat.

Feeding fresh foods

Eating salads and fresh fruit every day helps keep you healthy. These foods are full of nutrients. Just like you, your guinea pigs need to eat fresh foods. Give them fruit and vegetables from the kitchen, and collect wild plants. But be careful! Some wild plants are poisonous. Look on this page to identify some of the wild plants that are safe for your pets to eat.

Grass

Sorrel

Clover

Dandelion

Plantain

Wild plant food
Twice a week, gather a few handfuls of grass and safe weeds to feed your guinea pigs. You can also let them graze on fresh grass and plants (see p. 39).

(see p. 39)

Good food game
Try hiding your guinea pigs' food in a brick, or under a heap of hay. Fresh food smells very strongly. Your guinea pigs will have fun sniffing it out.

Clever guinea pig has found the food

This guinea pig smells the food but doesn't see it

⚘ Food must be fresh
Fresh plants, fruit, and vegetables quickly become stale. Throw away these foods if they haven't been eaten by bedtime. Never give your guinea pigs grass cuttings, because they go moldy very quickly.

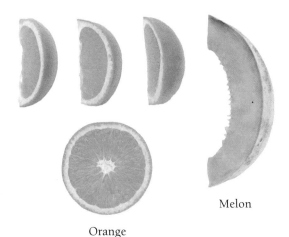

Orange

Pear

Apple

Grapes

Tomato

Melon

Favorite fruit
🐹🐹 Feed one slice of fresh fruit to each of your guinea pigs every day. Apple and pear slices may be chopped into small pieces to make them easier to nibble.

Crunchy vegetables
🐹🐹 Every day, chop up a handful of vegetables to give to each of your guinea pigs. Your greengrocer may be able to give you scraps that are suitable. Make sure they are fresh.

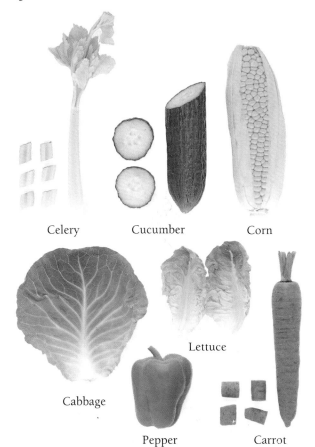

Celery   Cucumber   Corn

Cabbage

Lettuce

Pepper   Carrot

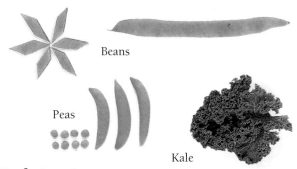

Beans

Peas

Kale

Vital vitamin
Just like you, guinea pigs need vitamin C to keep them healthy. Make sure you feed your guinea pigs a food that is rich in vitamin C every day. Give each one a quarter of an orange or a large handful of fresh cabbage or kale.

Cleaning the hutch

Your guinea pigs like their home to be very clean. If their hutch becomes dirty, it will start to smell, and your guinea pigs may become ill. You should clean out the hutch and wash the feeding equipment every day. Put new paper and fresh bedding, hay, food, and water in the hutch when you have finished. Once a week, scrub the hutch out thoroughly.

Don't forget to take out the bowls

Put the guinea pigs bottom first into the box

1 **Every day, put your pets** into their carrying box, one by one. This will keep them safely out of the way so you can clean their hutch. On a nice day, you could let them graze outside in their grazing ark (see p. 39).

Door opens wide so you can reach to clean

Sweep up uneaten food with the bedding

Remember to pull up all the old paper

Rubber gloves keep your hands clean

2 **Use your dustpan and brush** to sweep up old bedding, droppings, and stale food. Remember to wear your rubber gloves. Lift up all the lining paper. Throw everything away.

Do not scrape too hard, or you will damage the wood

Washing bowls
Wipe out each of the food bowls with the cleaning cloth. You might need to soak them if they are very dirty. Dry them with a paper towel.

Wipe right into the corners

3 Use your scraper to lift off any bits stuck to the floor or sides of the hutch. The corners are often dirtiest. Sweep up with the dustpan and brush.

Clearing the dropper
Make sure nothing is blocking the bottle dropper. Brush the tube with the spout brush. Then shake the tube. You should hear the metal ball moving around.

Twist the brush inside the tube

Spray to kill germs

Bucket with hot water and a squirt of detergent

Turn the brush to clean the inside

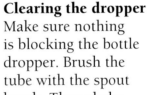

Cleaning the bottle
Pour hot, soapy water into the water bottle. Scrub the sides with the bottle brush. Rinse out the water bottle before filling it with fresh water.

Thorough cleaning
Once a week, use a brush and hot, soapy water to scrub the inside of the hutch. Rinse the hutch and then spray it with disinfectant. Leave it to dry out.

Grooming your guinea pigs

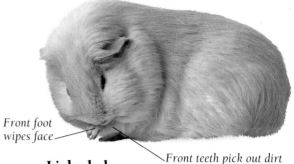

Brush your guinea pigs every day so that they get used to you petting them and handling them. Long-haired and rough-haired guinea pigs get dirt and hay stuck in their coats. Grooming keeps the hair clean and tangle-free. Wash your pets if their coats become smelly and greasy.

Front foot wipes face

Front teeth pick out dirt

Licked clean
A guinea pig spends a lot of time grooming itself. It uses its front teeth as a comb and its tongue as a washcloth. It can also use its back claws as combs.

Brushing all over
To groom a long-haired guinea pig, brush the hair on its back away from its head. Then brush its belly and under its chin.

Brush the hair in the direction it grows

Use one hand to keep your guinea pig still

Tell your guinea pig not to be afraid!

Put one hand on its back

Place one hand underneath the pig to support it

Dishpan

Combing the coat
After brushing, change to using the comb. Comb the back, and then under the chin. Untangle knots with your fingers.

Pull the comb gently through the hair

1 **To wash a guinea pig**, first lower it carefully into a bowl filled with a little warm water. It may wriggle, so hold on firmly.

2 Splash water onto the coat, but keep the face dry. Pour a capful of the special shampoo onto the back. Rub it into the coat with the tips of your fingers.

Rub shampoo in underneath as well as on top

Guinea pig looks white and foamy

Shampoo is from the veterinarian

3 Give your guinea pig a shower to rinse it. Pour warm water from the jug over its neck. Rub the water into its coat. Keep pouring and rubbing until there are no more bubbles in the coat.

Jug filled with warm water

Hold the head up high so the suds run off the back

4 Put your guinea pig onto the towel. Before it shakes itself and soaks you, quickly fold the towel around it. Rub your pet dry. When you unfold the towel, all its hair will be standing up. Brush and comb the hair gently.

Rub the coat all over with the towel

5 Put your guinea pig in the carrying box. Wrap the hot water bottle in a clean towel. Put the bottle in the box to keep the guinea pig warm. Place the box in a warm room. When the guinea pig is completely dry, put it back in the hutch.

Hot water bottle covered in a towel

Hay makes a cozy bed

Understanding guinea pigs

Guinea pigs show their mood by moving parts of their bodies. They mark the things that belong to them with their scent. They make lots of noises, from a purr to a squeal. Watch them, and you will soon understand what they are doing.

Nose sniffs the air

Eyes search

Neck is stretched

Sniffing

Smelly clues

Guinea pigs sniff the air to discover if there is anyone else close by. When two guinea pigs meet, they smell each other to find out if they are friends. They may sniff the other guinea pig's nose, or its bottom.

Sniffing the bottom of a stranger to see if it's friendly

Sniffing bottoms

Marking what's mine

Just like you, your guinea pigs label the things they own. Instead of writing their names on them, they leave their scent. The scent is in the skin on their cheeks, backs, and bottoms. It is also in the grease that comes from the grease gland at the base of the back.

Nose picks up other guinea pig's scent

Sniffing nose to nose

Dragging bottom

Scent is left as bottom slides along the ground

Rubbing cheeks

Scent is left on other guinea pig's cheek

Marking with grease

Grease is rubbed onto log

Still as a statue

Guinea pigs are very shy. When they hear a strange or loud sound, they do not move. Every hair on their body lies still. They think that if they freeze, an enemy won't spot them.

Fur is unruffled

Fur bristles up

Eyes stare at enemy

Angry guinea pig

Head twists away in fear

Timid guinea pig

Meeting the enemy

A guinea pig can get angry with another guinea pig. Its hair stands on end to make it look bigger. It makes a loud chattering sound to tell the other pig that it is annoyed.

The angry guinea pig

When a guinea pig becomes furious, it yawns to show its razor-sharp teeth.

Mouth opens wide to show teeth

The boxing match

If both guinea pigs are brave, they will fight. They stand on their back legs and ram each other with their heads. They keep their mouths open, ready to bite.

Ears are perked up

Hair stands on end

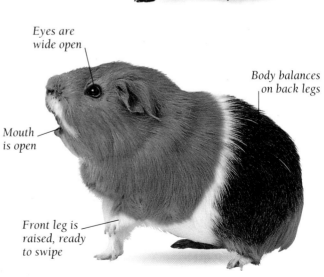

Eyes are wide open

Body balances on back legs

Mouth is open

Front leg is raised, ready to swipe

The enclosure

Guinea pigs love to be outside. Ask an adult to fence off a grassy area of your yard to make an enclosure. Stand the hutch in a corner. Put things in the area for your guinea pigs to play with. Make a ramp so your pets can climb down from the hutch.

Bottle filled with fresh water

Guinea pig hides in large pipe

Rocks to hide behind

Clay pipe to run through

Small log to gnaw

Holes in brick make a perfect hiding place for food

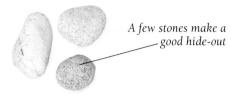

A few stones make a good hide-out

Things to collect
Try to find bricks, stones, and clay pipes to put in the enclosure. Guinea pigs love to explore new things.

Beware of these dangers

Plastic sheet can be pulled over area when it rains

Wire mesh protects area from other animals

Prowling cats may jump into the area.

Birds of prey may swoop down.

Weedkillers on the grass are poisonous to guinea pigs.

Dogs may scare your guinea pigs.

Some plants will poison guinea pigs.

Bright sun and bad weather might make your guinea pigs ill.

Carrot to nibble

Rungs on the ramp stop guinea pigs from slipping

The guinea pig enclosure
It is fun to watch your guinea pigs play in the enclosure. Try to understand what they are doing (see p. 34). If you're not inside the enclosure, cover it with mesh to prevent other animals from getting in. Protect the area with plastic if it rains.

37

Things to do with your pets

Look in magazines about pets, or ask your veterinarian for the address of your local guinea pig club. If you join the junior section, you can talk to other guinea pig owners about exciting things to do with your pets. Everyone will have good ideas to help you make a fun box and a grazing ark.

Showing your guinea pigs
You can take your guinea pigs to a guinea pig show. The judge will give prizes to the pet guinea pigs that are cared for the best.

Rosette for the winning owner

Groomed coat looks beautiful

The indoor fun box
👥 Ask an adult to help you make a fun box. Fill it with wooden and paper things for your guinea pigs to play with. Put your pets in their fun box every day. If your guinea pigs can't play in an enclosure or ark, you must let them exercise in their fun box for at least an hour every day.

Gently lower your guinea pigs backward into the box

Fresh water for a drink during play

Pieces of fruit and vegetables to eat

Shredded paper makes a cozy bed

Cardboard tube to wriggle through

Each side must be at least 8 in. (20 cm.) high

Hay spread over floor

Ramp to climb up and down

Cut-up shoe box makes a good playhouse

Small branch to gnaw on

Bowl filled with dried food

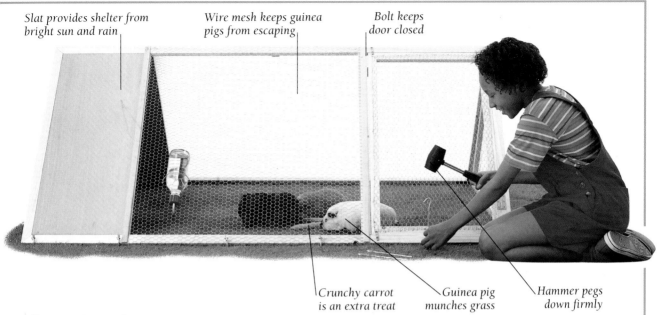

Slat provides shelter from bright sun and rain

Wire mesh keeps guinea pigs from escaping

Bolt keeps door closed

Crunchy carrot is an extra treat

Guinea pig munches grass

Hammer pegs down firmly

The grazing ark

In dry weather, you can put your guinea pigs out on grass in a grazing ark for an hour a day. Peg the ark down so that your guinea pigs can't tip it up, and other animals can't get inside. Move the ark every day, so your guinea pigs always have fresh grass to nibble.

Leaving your guinea pigs

Going on vacation
You can't always take your guinea pigs with you when you go on vacation. You must find someone to take care of them. You may have a friend with guinea pigs who has time to look after yours as well.

Making a checklist
Make a list of the jobs that need doing every day. Write them down in the order that you do them. Your guinea pigs are used to this order and may be upset if your friend changes it. Make a note of the name and telephone number of your veterinarian.

What to pack
Get everything ready for your friend. Make sure you pack enough food. Don't forget all the cleaning and grooming equipment.

Moving your guinea pigs
Take your guinea pigs to your friend in their carrying box or small cage. Bring their fun box or grazing ark if your friend has nowhere for your pets to exercise.

Having babies

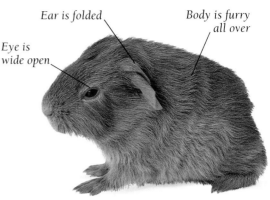

Just as women can have children, female guinea pigs can have baby guinea pigs, called puppies. Think carefully before keeping female and male pigs together, because they will breed. Remember that you will have to find good homes for all of the puppies. Your veterinarian may be able to give your guinea pigs a neutering operation. This stops them from having babies, but doesn't harm them.

Ear is folded

Body is furry all over

Eye is wide open

Miniature adult
A newborn puppy looks like a tiny grown-up. It has a full coat and its eyes are open. It can crawl around after a few minutes, and eats solid food when it is four days old.

❖ Responsible owner
It may seem fun to let your guinea pigs have puppies, but don't forget that these cuddly balls of fluff soon grow up. You will need to find each of them a good home.

1 The newborns drink milk from their mother. There can be as many as four puppies. Because the mother has only two nipples, just two puppies can drink at a time.

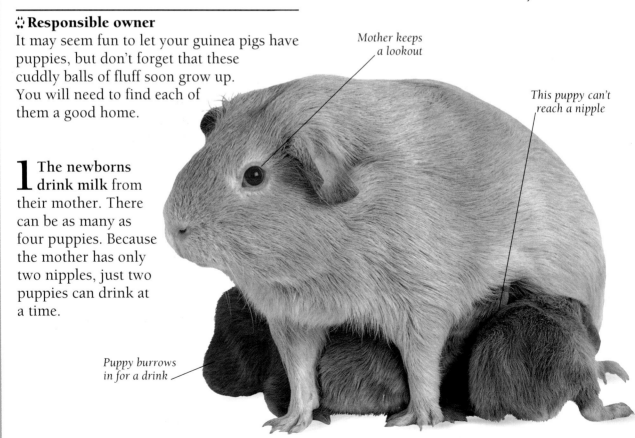

Mother keeps a lookout

This puppy can't reach a nipple

Puppy burrows in for a drink

This bold puppy climbs on top

Puppy cuddles up to keep warm

Puppy looks for its brothers and sisters

2 **At two weeks old**, the puppies hate to be apart. They make a purring sound to tell one another where they are, and all huddle together to keep warm. They will drink milk from their mother until they are three weeks old.

Eye searches around

Ear listens out

3 **When the puppies are five weeks old**, they are very curious. They are nearly old enough to have babies of their own. The males and females must be kept apart because they are not old enough to make good parents.

Pinkish gray coat

Eye is deep pink

Nose sniffs curiously

4 **A five-month-old guinea pig** is almost fully grown. Both males and females are now ready to have a family of their own. Keep them apart unless you want your guinea pigs to breed.

Fur is thick and sleek

5 **As a guinea pig grows older**, its body becomes plump. It needs to have at least one friend. You should always keep it with another guinea pig of the same sex.

Grown-up guinea pig has plump body

Health care

You need to look after your guinea pigs properly to make sure they stay fit and healthy. You should give them the right food (see p. 26), keep them well groomed (p. 32), and clean out their hutch regularly (p. 30). You also need to do some simple health checks with your guinea pigs every day. You will learn to spot quickly if one is unwell. If you think something is wrong, take it to your veterinarian immediately.

Hold guinea pig steady with one hand

1 **Check your guinea pig's coat** is in good condition. Push the fur backward so you can see down to the skin. The fur should feel soft and smell clean. Don't forget to check the belly, and hidden places, like between the back legs.

Read how much your guinea pig weighs

Put paper in the tray to keep it clean

2 **Weigh your guinea pig** at the same time, on the same day, every week. Write down the results. Wash the weighing tray thoroughly afterward. If your guinea pig has lost or gained weight, it may be ill, or it may not be getting enough exercise.

Look down
the ear hole

Pull back the
fur around
the ear

3 Examine your guinea pig's ears and eyes. The ears should look clean, and the eyes should be bright and shiny.

Claw is
too long

Claw is
correct
length

4 Check that your guinea pig's claws are not too long. Gently pick up each foot between your finger and thumb. Look to see if the claws are the right length.

Pull back
the lips with
your fingers

5 👫 To look at your pet's teeth, put it on its back in your lap. Pull the lips away, being sure to keep your fingers back. The teeth should look clean, white, short, and straight.

Cleaning the grease gland

Male guinea pigs may get a sticky patch of fur on their backs. The stickiness comes from the grease gland. Clean it off with soapy water, then rinse it.

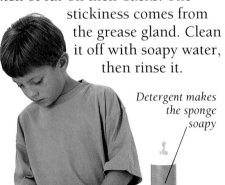

Detergent makes
the sponge
soapy

Wipe with a
soapy sponge

Your pet care checklist

Use this list to keep a record of all the jobs you need to do.

Copy this chart. Check off the jobs when you have finished them.

Every day:

Feed your pets

Wash the bowls

Wash and fill bottle

Change bedding

Spread new paper

Put down fresh hay

Groom your pigs

Put your pets in the enclosure for at least an hour

Look at coat

Check ears and eyes

Examine claws

Check teeth length

◆

Once a week:

Scrub the hutch

Weigh your pets

Check grease gland

Tidy the enclosure

Clean the fun box

Check food and bedding supplies

◆

Every year:

Take your guinea pigs to the veterinarian for a full check-up

Visiting the veterinarian

The veterinarians and veterinary assistants who work at your local vet's office want to help you keep your guinea pigs happy and healthy. They will tell you how to care for your pets properly. You can ask them as many questions as you like. They will also try to make your pets better when they are ill.

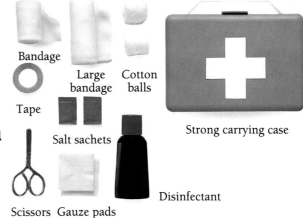

Bandage

Large bandage

Cotton balls

Tape

Salt sachets

Strong carrying case

Scissors Gauze pads

Disinfectant

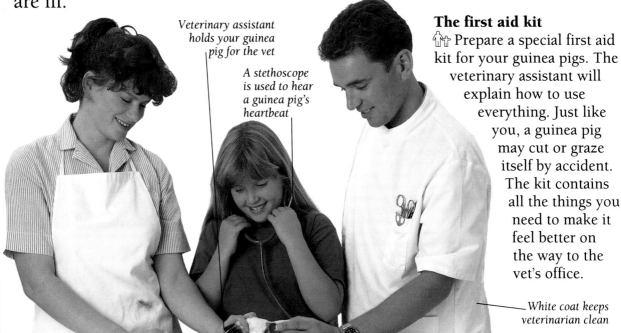

Veterinary assistant holds your guinea pig for the vet

A stethoscope is used to hear a guinea pig's heartbeat

The first aid kit

Prepare a special first aid kit for your guinea pigs. The veterinary assistant will explain how to use everything. Just like you, a guinea pig may cut or graze itself by accident. The kit contains all the things you need to make it feel better on the way to the vet's office.

White coat keeps veterinarian clean

Your veterinary assistant
Your veterinary assistant helps your veterinarian. She knows a lot about guinea pigs. When you have any questions about your guinea pigs, visit or call her.

Your veterinarian
Your veterinarian gives your guinea pig special health checks. If your pet is ill, he will tell you what needs to be done to make it better. He may give you medicine for your pet.

My pet's fact sheet

Try making a fact sheet about your pet guinea pigs. Copy the headings on this page, or you can make up your own. Then write in the correct information about each of your guinea pigs.

White stripe
Brown ear
Black eye
Rough coat

Leave a space to stick in a photograph or draw a picture of each of your pets. Then label all of your pet's special features.

Name: Splash

Birthday: March 9

Weight: 2 pounds (900 grams)

Favorite fresh food: Cucumber

Best friend: Susie

Veterinarian's name: Mark Evans

Veterinary assistant's name: Thaddeus Weir

Vet's office telephone number: 555-1234

Index